MY WALLET
AFTER 20 YEARS

MONEY ADVICE EVERY YOUNG FILIPINO SHOULD KNOW

YOLI ANGELES

MY WALLET

AFTER 20 YEARS

MONEY ADVICE EVERY YOUNG FILIPINO SHOULD KNOW

YOLI ANGELES

My Wallet After 20 Years
Money Advice Every Young Filipino Should Know

Copyright © 2021 by
Yoli Angeles
ISBN 978-621-8125-73-5
First edition, December 2021

The information in this book was obtained from the author's research, personal experiences, and insights. While every effort has been made to make this book as accurate as possible, the author disclaims any liability or risk as a direct or indirect consequence of the use of the contents of this book.

Furthermore, the views and opinions of the author do not necessarily represent the views and opinions of the publisher.

Cover Design, Editing, and Layout by Mae Gomez & Team

Published by: Write Conversations Publishing and Consultancy

Address requests for information to
write@seminarphilippines.com
Printed in the Philippines.

DEDICATION

This book is dedicated

to all young Filipino professionals.

I have the highest hopes for all of you.

"Yoli is the real deal when it comes to saving and investing! Her book is an eye-opener especially to the young professionals today who seem unwary of their financial future. She's friendly and you can tell that she cares about you and lead you to a path to financial success through her book. She provides simple and effective financial advice whether you are a newbie or an old-timer. You inspire a lot of people!"

MARK GERARD SALVADOR
Stock Market Investor
The Investing Engineer
https://investingengineer.com

"It is of great privilege to hold her first book on financial literacy for young people. She talks of wealth that comes first from values and self-discipline to avoid falling into debt. I assure the readers of Yoli's book that you will thank yourself soon when you appropriately prepare and act NOW."

JEISEL O. LABATETE
Financial Advisor

"Yoli has finally written a simple must-read guidebook on financial literacy, especially for young professionals. I'm truly impressed with how she conveys herself in her book by prompting readers to rewire their brains to save and invest as early as possible."

CHRISTIAN JAY P. WATSON
Young Investing Professional

"If I could only go back 20 years ago when I started earning on my own, I wish I got hold of this book. *My Wallet After 20 Years* provides a good start for every young Filipino who wishes to maximize every single peso at an early stage in life."

DARWIN M. APISTAR
Financial Advisor

ACKNOWLEDGMENTS

The completion of this book was made possible by the patience and guidance of my coach, Sha T. Nacino, one of Asia's book writing trainers, a trusted global keynote speaker on gratitude, happiness, and productivity, a corporate mentor, and an author of 15 books.

I also wish to thank the following:

My book cover designer, editor, and layout artist, Mae E. Gomez and her team for the remarkable design and editing of this book;

My former student, Jeisel O. Labatete, who as young as she is, chose to be a financial advisor. I salute her;

Darwin M. Apistar, a longtime colleague and also a financial advisor, for promoting this book;

Mark Gerard Salvador, my mentor in stocks investing who patiently guided when I started in the market and who also advertised this book;

Christian Jay P. Watson, my colleague and example of a young professional who values youthful investing, thank you too for recommending this work;

My *unica iha* Yvoney Freya, my mother Lolita, my siblings and my husband who were all my silent pillars throughout, family, friends and everyone else who helped me one way or another, my earnest thanks to all of you.

TABLE OF CONTENTS

TABLE OF CONTENTS

Tired of Always Borrowing Money?

By Sha Nacino

When I was in my first year as an employee, I got buried in credit card debts. I can clearly remember that day when I only had Php50 in my wallet and my salary was 3 days away.

It was almost lunchtime, I was hungry, but I didn't have enough money to buy myself lunch. I was shy to borrow from office mates. I took out my cell phone and called up my Papa who's based in the province, some 12 hours away from Manila.

"Pa, can I borrow Php1,000?"

In less than an hour, my father sent me the money via LBC. He wanted to increase the amount, but I assured him that Php1,000 would be fine.

From my office in Ayala Avenue, I walked all the way to Buendia with my high heels. I had to traverse the stretch of Buendia to locate LBC and get my Php1,000 so I could buy lunch! I had no umbrella, and the heat of the sun melted my make-up. I felt like a foolish clown who was on the verge of crying. Had there been cameras around, the scene would have been perfect for a funny, melo-dramatic music video.

My Papa — wise and loving — knew how to give support and a powerful lesson at the same time. His words hit me. "Sha, at the rate that you're spending, you'll go bankrupt in no time. You should have a conscious effort to manage your money."

Papa very rarely gives me unsolicited advice. He has always been vocal about how pleased he is having me as his daughter. When he said those words, he must have been serious... and so I took his words seriously.

That literally got me started to invest in my financial education. It's a continuing education with no graduation. I'm glad a lot of things have changed since then.

Today, I have my own business. My investments are doing well. Best of all, I'm living the life I've always dreamed of.

Did you ever experience eating your pride and borrowing money from a friend or officemate? It must be painful.

Are you getting little sleep worried over your credit card debts?

Do you want to retire early but you can't — because you still have debts that will shrink your retirement to almost nothing?

What must be the solution?

Earning more money doesn't guarantee financial success. The game-changer is education, specifically, financial education. Financial Literacy was never really taught in school; so, we have a lot of catching up to do. It's okay. Today is always the best time to learn; not tomorrow, not yesterday.

The good news is, there are so many ways to invest in financial literacy. One is by reading great books on money management.

In this book, Yoli shares her tips on how she was able to zero out her debts as well as her tips on saving and investing. If you want to zero out your debts and free yourself from financial worries, this book can help you.

I know Yoli through my signature online course The 90-Day Book Writing Challenge.

I am glad she wrote this book.

Enjoy!

Sha Nacino

Author of 15 books
Founder, The 90-Day Book Writing Challenge
(shanacino.com/write)

INTRODUCTION

Dear Young Filipino Reader,

First, let's sit down together.

Relax and find yourself sitting down with me somewhere in the corner of a coffee shop, cold and cozy with a strong and soothing aroma of immersing ground coffee beans from the 'mountains of Madagascar of the Philippines,' the Mt. Province. While waiting for the brewing coffee that we requested, let's talk about financial education first. I will tell you about my financial life as a wage earner for over two decades, what I exactly witnessed in the world of being an employee and what lessons I need to share with the young Filipino professionals today.

Let's begin...

"The Philippines has a financial literacy problem!" This statement comes from the Business World newspaper released in July 2019. The same is mentioned in a study made by the Bangko Sentral ng Pilipinas (BSP) cited by the World Bank in 2015, that Filipinos lack specific knowledge about financial education.

A lot of financial literacy programs are available these days, but it seems these are perpetually camouflaged so that only a few financially wise can see them. Young Filipinos seem to be more knowledgeable about the latest trends on HOW TO SPEND like getting credit cards, when mall sales occur, and getting loans as well as cheap but long-term installments on gadgets, rather than WHERE TO SAVE AND INVEST! How about helping these youth understand these literacy programs to avoid high levels of early debt and instead, save and invest. Lack of financial literacy opens the doors to borrowing more and saving less, therefore, ending up paying more rates that eventually leads to bankruptcy, or worse, misery.

Why is it so important to learn about financial literacy at a young age? First, remember that it helps the youth to effectively manage a budget, choose the right financial products, and prepare for life events, including buying a house or retirement. Financial literacy is not a skill just for middle-aged or old people, but it is a skill that every young professional must possess. It is a fundamental life skill that empowers one to make smart economic decisions and be able to play a part in modern society. It provides the knowledge and skills one needs to manage money effectively in budgeting, saving, borrowing and investing. This means that one would be better equipped to reach financial goals and achieve financial stability. Second, children are growing up in a world that is increasingly changing where they will eventually need to take charge of their financial future. The way of earning is increasingly changing also. National surveys all around the world show that young adults have the lowest levels of financial literacy.

I am not an economics graduate nor an expert in financial jargon and not even one among the renowned financial advisors. But what I want to share through this book is how to at least manage your lives given whatever amount you are earning.

I made wrong turns throughout my youth as an employee and I don't want the young readers to make the same mistakes. This book was written and intended to guide not only the young generation these days but anyone, to understand what salary is alone. I am an exact example of having wasted years because I didn't know how to invest! My greatest regret in life was I did not invest when I was in my 20's to early 30's! Nobody influenced and taught me during my younger years to recalibrate my brains to wise investing. There's a dire need today, therefore, for anyone to be taught the maxim, "you must save and invest!"

Yes, many young people will not and will never agree with me now because of their principles of spending and enjoying while they are still able. These millennials will mostly argue that they won't enjoy things when they get old, i.e., traveling, eating out, owning cars, and dressing expensively. Besides, why think of those sunset years when time is still too young! Just enjoy while the physiques are able! Life is so short so enjoy they say. Well, yes, you earned your own money and you owe it to yourselves! That's not a problem. Remember however, that you also deserve to retire well! You and I won't deny that we can't stop time nor ask it to wait for us. We hate it but that is the fact. We are growing older every day, and will all eventually grow physically old and become weak therefore we need to foresee what may happen along the way. You will not enjoy your golden years if you don't have money anymore. What if you live long but not have prepared for it? Would you oblige your children or anyone to financially take care of you? Rainy days along the way surely would come and if not geared up well, financial problems would blow pockets off to tatters. This is what I want to impart – to break that cycle for you! If you are earning while taking care of your parents and at the same time taking care of children (if you have already a family), it would be very, very difficult to save for investments if this is the situation. However, it is not impossible.

I would like to ask this question to every young Filipino professional today: Are you financially satisfied and confident that you will live an economically stable life later especially when you retire? If your answer is no, then read on, this book is for you.

CHAPTER ONE

RUNNING THE RAT RACE

*"If you want to be financially free,
you need to become a different
person than you are today and let
go of whatever has held you back
in the past." — Robert Kiyosaki*

My Finances for the Last 30 Years

"How much now is your bank savings?"

"Good for you because you already have a lot of investments."

These were comments I would always dread hearing. Many times, I just wish to become invisible at the very moment because I didn't want more questions or comments that I cannot answer nor interpret. Thinking about it though, I had been an employee for 30 years, yet I did not have any bank savings. That was the truth! Plus, I nurtured strings of debt that I needed to face every month.

Though during my first years of employment as I was immediately hired after graduation at 20, I had to help with the family budget. It is typical of Filipino culture for older children to financially help in the family once capable of earning. I am the eldest of a brood of eight that time when I graduated from college, so I felt obliged to help send my younger siblings to college also. (I was able to finance the college expenses of one of my siblings simultaneously with another who took a two-year vocational course.) I was only earning a few pesos per day during those years and there was barely anything left for me. But just to carry on with life, I had to do the stressful jobs that my superiors wanted me to accomplish and report them every month to the head office. The program where I worked for 7 years was time-bounded and foreign-funded. Thus, when it was completed, all direct employees were co-terminated. Though I was one of the two luckiest who was chosen to stay with the program's mother bureau after the termination, I had to resign after 6 months. I was not happy with my new assignment.

I then tried luck in the second-hand clothing business for just a few months after my resignation. But as the usual problem in small-scale businesses, struggling with rents, permits, and everything else makes one drained due to frustration.

Finally, I found another job in a different region. Immediately, I landed a permanent position in the government. The salary was not so attractive including the location of my newfound work, but I had to wrestle with my new situation. Having been born and have grown in a temperate climate with a very different social upbringing was not only physically consuming but emotionally draining as well when I moved to my new tropical environment. But since I needed a job, I had to adjust. I needed money. I needed to survive.

I was nearly 29 when our youngest sister was born! She was a menopausal baby. As the eldest, and as if it was part of my guilty feelings, the sense of responsibility to help the family survive the daily battle continued enduring within me. Though I was so indignant about the birth of our little sister at that time, I needed to do something because I knew that my other siblings would not be able to fully take on the responsibility of financially helping her to college if the time comes. I finished college on my own and it was a life full of difficulty thus I didn't want her to go through the same. That time, my parents' temperate fruit tree orchard was at its height of production so I asked my mother if she could save an amount from her sales every quarter and I would add up another 35% to deposit for a college educational plan.

When my baby sister was a year old, I gave birth to my daughter too. I also bought an educational plan for her. Paying a quarterly amount for my own daughter's and adding 35% for my mother's payment was taxing my pockets. It was a risk. Paying for two was a heavy financial burden. But, sixteen years after, my mother started to reap what was saved during those earlier years.

It was unfortunate though that the Pre-Need Company we invested in started to go bankrupt and was already on the brink of collapse exactly at the time when the pandemic hurt the global as well as the country's economy. The pandemic struck the company more to a sorry state. My mother was able to receive all the amount due her in the middle of the pandemic and we were thankful enough. For my part, my daughter's policy was affected so that I lost 23% of the total amount I should have received plus an extension of 5 years waiting did not sit well for me of that company. Understanding investment, however, is prone to risk. An appetite for higher gain means higher risk. I could still tell myself that it was a gain after all, even if not so satisfying as what I chased 20 years back.

An Employee Tirelessly Running in Circles

Working with the government does not always promise an attractive salary. Still, many aspire be a government employee because of the notion of job stability and that many benefits are accompanying the wage. True, I worked for 30 years in the government but what did I have?

On several occasions, I would find myself reincarnating memories of my sprightly youth then afterward quietly asking myself several what ifs. My mind never stopped asking so many questions and many times too I would find blaming myself for the many bad decisions and mistakes I've made and committed.

Alone one cool evening, I went to a place under some tall trees and sat down listening to the rushing happy brook nearby and the jubilant sunset choral of birds above me. Here I began to evaluate myself and as usual, felt that meagerness once again then started questioning the years I have already lost in my workplace. I kept telling myself that I was so stupid of the several things I did that lead to my deep feelings of inadequacy. I questioned my financial status, of what had I been doing! Being a phlegmatic-sanguine person and having mild ADHD may have contributed to my current state, however. My salary was still below 30,000 a month and that was already in 2016. I was already 17 years holding a permanent position in the government! I told myself that I just wasted my adult life on nothing. I was paid regularly, but I felt I had accomplished nothing back since I always dreamt of leaving even a modest legacy to my workplace upon retirement (lots and lots of shenanigans in the system of my very own work organization though were among the numerous factors). But what did I do with all those years for myself, my organization, my family, my community?

While working, I did some small trades to augment my salary but whatever did I do so that I ended up with no bank savings, no satisfying investments, no nothing! I was able though to purchase a small lot back in 2011 thankful enough because I paid it through installment for five years. But my scheme was, every time I paid a bigger amount, I had to apply for a mortgage that earned interest so that the supposed total amount of the lot was not the actual amount I paid because of the interest rates of the payments I made from loans. In short, I didn't know what I was doing with the purchase of that investment! I was glad though I finally owned it.

I cannot help but financially compare myself to my childhood friends, classmates, clan members, college and postgraduate friends who some of them occupy well-compensated positions in their workplaces as directors, executives, etc., I feel so differentiated. Some are happy working and traveling abroad, some successful business people, and still, some are happy with their own families and have successful children. I can see all their achievements. And here I am in the Philippines working for the country but have no house yet of my own and no car for comfortable living. For whom then did I bring my salaries? I also do not know. I only remember that it may have melted down the road to food, clothing, and many items that were not so necessary.

I continued to be just an ordinary employee taking home pay of 5 digits with an uncertain financial future.

What I Continue to Witness

Society is composed of a staircase age grouping. Some are children, some young adults, some middle-aged, some are old and still, some are older. Ever since the time I was a very young government servant, I always witnessed up to this day how new incoming young employees, as well as outgoing or retirees, fared with life. What only raises alarm was I always see retiring employees who had been in positions, well-salaried during their vibrant years, (some involved in corrupt practices) but usually had to fight with the housing authorities particularly for extension of housing benefits from the agency that they enjoyed earlier. Why did they end up that way of having nowhere to go after the mandatory retiring age? It's all because they never prepared for their sunset years. They were "millionaires" during their sunnier days. They had a lifestyle thinking that years will never encounter bleak days. Others were scammed because of hypnotic promises of swindlers they got wedged upon retirement. Others who lived longer beyond the mandatory retirement age were forced to solicit for maintenance. Still, others had to sell most of their properties and ended up nothing. Instead of enjoying their retirement days, others even had to continue working to the extent of joining the world of ambulant vending. These were and are continuing to be the sad truths that most Filipinos who had no financial education mostly end up to. Witnessing and knowing these situations, I still never learned though! And being in between a phlegmatic-sanguine temperament, I was contented with just what the day brought me - a single source of income – salary! Which in later years, realized it was so insufficient after all, the reason I thought of at least sharing a piece of advice to the employed youth – not to repeat the same financial position that many and I have experienced.

CHAPTER TWO

OF SAVING AND INVESTING

"Knowledge is power: you hear it all the time, but knowledge is not power. It's only potential power. It only becomes power when we apply it and use it. Somebody who reads a book and doesn't apply it, they're at no advantage over someone illiterate. None of it works unless you work. We have to do our part. If knowing is half the battle, action is the second half of the battle." — Jim Kwik

"Financial freedom is available to those who learn about it and work for it."
— Robert Kiyosaki

How I Learned to Invest

I mentioned earlier that I was an employee for over 20 years without much savings and investments. But as one avid reader of stories hence keeping collections of all sorts including self-help paperbacks, it took me decades before I finally settled to reading books on saving and investing. Between 2011 to 2012, I was coached to a networking business on food supplements. It was here where I was first ushered to financial self-help books like that of Robert Kiyosaki's Rich Dad, Poor Dad, and his Rich Dad's Cashflow Quadrant A Guide to Financial Freedom. I learned a lot from his financial pearls of wisdom in these books. I may have been gradually and subconsciously brainwashed from the insights from these books so that somehow in very minute ways, I got influenced – however, in knowledge only! Several years later, as my habit, if free, I still go to surplus bookshops and other bookstores so that it was by the end of 2016 that I got attracted to an investing guidebook on display at the National Bookstore authored by Fitzgerard Villafuerte. However expensive for me at that time, I still bought one copy. I read through every page from conditioning the mind for wealth to learning how to save money, budgeting, and zeroing in debts to getting life insurance and to smart investing goals. Those topics were discussed on the first 1/3 of the whole pages of the book. When I came to the section of different types of investments like bonds, mutual funds, UITFs, real estate, and stocks, I didn't understand anything! I am an agriculturist by profession dealing with biology so what did I know about those fiscal terms! I admit, I just skipped those pages and read a portion on building an emergency fund which I understood a bit. Later, I bought another self-help book purely on the stock market written by Marvin Germo. What did not sit well on my understanding was about investments in stocks, bonds, mutual funds, and UITFs! The phrase "stock market" had been passing by my sight on printed dailies before but never did I have any idea of what it was until I found the book.

A few more years went by and by following Villafuerte and Germo's guide, I was able to zero in with debts following their first step which was by listing all daily expenses. This was to monitor where money was being spent and to identify where to adjust a budget. I keep a journal of this kind to this day. Finally, although it took me five years, I was able to fully announce that I was set free from debt, debt that I practiced over and over in a span of over 20 years while being an employee!

It was towards the end of 2020, the first year of the pandemic when people were trying to find alternatives of survival that I came across a title of a booklet on social media "How to Invest: Three Simple Steps" that can be downloaded free provided one signs up through email. It was offering a piece of financial advice. I signed in since I got attracted to the title alone, leaving only my alternative email address with the author. Immediately, I received a reply. It was from Mr. Mark Gerard Salvador, an electrical engineer by profession. His booklet was a short one, a direct guide on becoming a member and investing in the Philippine Stock Exchange through the COL Financial Philippines. He further introduced becoming a member with Bo Sanchez's, The Truly Rich Club, a stock market guide. That time, I just also signed up to become a member of the International Marketing Group (IMG), a financial education organization, and a vehicle for paper investments. Both financial vehicles required membership fees that one cannot just simply and readily shell out from his pockets. Following the guide of Mr. Mark, I signed up through the COL Financial Philippines, free. I communicated with him on how the COL works. Then he mentioned becoming a member of The Truly Rich Club. I was a bit hesitant because of the required fee. In the end though, again, I signed up. I emailed Mr. Mark and asked a few questions and on how he should guide me along. True enough, he was so supportive and even sent me a template of a budget planner as a bonus.

I may have already been saturated with enough knowledge on financial education from the time I first read Kiyosaki's two books, but it was myself who was the problem. The knowledge was already ripe with me, but I never started the ACTION. I just continued with my old financial way of living from paycheck to paycheck. Not until the pandemic and the convincing power of Mr. Mark Salvador that I had to learn to invest in paper assets.

First Steps I did in the COL Financial

Coupled with the financial education lectures I listened to from the IMG; I evaluated my appetite for investing. Without much reluctance, I followed Mr. Mark's step-by-step advice. Since I started investing in Mutual Funds through IMG, I also started investing in the stock market through COL Financial. I followed the advice of both by setting apart a small portion of my salary every month and investing in either mutual funds or stocks. I found that investing in the stock market was more challenging to my financial appetite than in mutual funds, so I tended to temporarily pause investing in the latter. I concentrated on investing small amounts in the former. It was in the stock market that I learned about how to wisely invest in it by following a vehicle or guide. Thanks again to the convincing power of Mr. Mark that I was able to sign up for membership in The Truly Rich Club Philippines founded by Bo Sanchez. It was through this vehicle that I was educated on strictly deciding to nail down discipline into my being. I was gradually brainwashed on how to separate needs from useless objects especially items on sale through the talks of guests in the TRC platform. What I so loved about the TRC is they have a lot of financial education materials that were easy to understand. They have frequent financial education talks delivered through webinars that furthered what I read from books and what I listened to from financial educators in the Philippines. They also teach when to buy and sell stocks and have chosen companies that perform well in the market so as not to lose money. As of this writing, it's a year since I invested in the Philippine Stock Exchange and I don't regret it. There's money in stocks. I use my earnings to buy more stocks and sell them at their target prices. With the series of lockdowns due to this pandemic, almost every company is plunging to cheap prices. It's a very opportune time to buy more stocks. This is the reason why financial educators repeatably advise stock investors to consider that investing should be in the long-term mindset because you must wait until the economy gets well again. And that money used for investing should be an extra amount in the budget that you can afford to lose without being so much affected.

Investing in the Stock Market

"The stock market is only for the rich."

"It is risky because you lose 85% of your money in the stocks."

These are commonly heard from people who know so little about investing in the stock market. We have to remember, however, that trading and investing in the stock market are both different stories. Most who lose money in the stock market are traders. The rule of TRC is investing in giant companies. Do not look at the stocks every day. It is recommended to check it while depositing into it every month. This is investing and just investing small amounts. Just small amounts. Buy a stock below its price and wait for the price to reach your target price. It requires you to change your behavior and wait patiently. Thus, this method of investing is called long-term because the waiting period may be counted as years. It is also called money cost averaging according to the TRC wherein one does the buy below price scheme for protection. It is not trading because trading is when a trader watches the stock market every hour or every day and buys and sells immediately. There are a lot of companies out there and if without knowledge of their backgrounds is where a lot of traders truly lose their money. That is why anyone who wants to engage in the stock market is to brainwash yourself that this is a LONG-TERM investment. It means to wait 10-20 years. This is the reason why I am recommending this piece for young employed people who are around their 20's to early 30's so by the time they reach 40-50 years old, then they can call themselves financially stable. Reaching 40-50 years old is also usually the age when our physical bodies start to feel things that need to be repaired and usually through medications then you have something to use. To the young people, please heed the advice of your financial advisors who gained a lot of pains just to survive and teach you today. You will soon become 40, 50, 60,70, and older and we don't want you to be in situations we had been earlier.

CHAPTER THREE

PRACTICAL TIPS FOR A HEALTHY WALLET

"Like all learning, financial education is a process that should begin at an early age and continue throughout life. This cumulative process builds the skills necessary for making critical financial decisions that affect one's ability to attain the assets, such as education, property, and savings, that improve economic well-being."
– Alan Greenspan, economist and former chair of the Federal Reserve of the United States

Although this book was written primarily for the young Filipino people who are already employed, these pieces of advice are also for anyone including OFWs who are earning a lot may be looking for some guidance about managing their earnings.

Here are some tips:

a.   **<u>SAVE SLOWLY but SURELY</u>**

Seriously embracing the attitude of a "self-imposed requirement" of saving a portion of whatever amount especially if you have a regular earning is something very worthwhile. The advice given by the TRC is to save at least 10-20% of the monthly income. Take for example a monthly income of 20,000.00 pesos. Ten percent of this amount is 2,000.00. If you think you cannot yet afford to save this amount because you may be currently zeroing in a debt, then you can adjust your saving at 5% which amounts to 1,000.00 pesos. This is already reasonable. The tip here is: SAVE AND FORGET! To have this kind of attitude is to nail down yourself of a pre-requisite that means SERIOUS SELF-DISCIPLINE! Whatever happens if not yet between life and death, then do not touch these savings. It will not disappear provided you did not put it in a scam. Just continuously deposit.

Build your finances and become financially independent so that when you grow old, you will not be a burden to your children.

b.   <u>BUILD an EMERGENCY FUND</u>

What does an emergency fund mean? This is money set aside to cover any unexpected financial or emergency that may cross your way that is stressful and costly. Examples of emergencies are job loss that exactly happened during the pandemic lockdowns, any medically related crises, deaths in the family, unexpected tuition fees or travel adjustments, etc.

I was recently talking to two young professionals in my workplace about savings and when I mentioned emergency funds, they were not aware of it. I imagined myself way back just like them when I didn't know these monetary terms. Today is 2021. I am talking to millennial professionals. Was I surprised? I'm not.

Time and again the Bangko Sentral ng Pilipinas (BSP) do surveys on the financial literacy status of

Filipinos and time and again it shows the same low trend which means time and again, Filipinos are illiterate when it comes to monetary education. In one interview, the governor of the BSP Benjamin E. Diokno said that many Filipinos are suffering from 'apparent financial insecurity' stemming from the lack of awareness of financial literacy, therefore, obstructing their ability to cope during crises.

Anyway, almost all financial educators would advise one to first and foremost build an emergency fund before attempting to set aside savings for investment. When I was reading Villafuerte's financial guidebook, I ran over and over through the pages where this was discussed to be sure that I understood well what it meant and how to apply it. Yes, it would really be very difficult to initiate yourself to do the action but once you deposit your first ever amount for an emergency fund, you will never regret that you did it. You will also experience a satisfying feeling of being a victor because you conquered yourself of doubts and fear. Congratulate yourself for that. The tip here is, find a good bank and open a passbook account, and do not ever link it to any online access so it wouldn't be so tempting to withdraw and use in unnecessary things. It is always advisable to use passbooks and do over-the-counter transactions rather than online. Do not also use an ATM card for emergency fund deposits since this is so easy to swipe wherever you are. Those small evils that reside in you will swiftly grow into big evils once you are in a very tempting situation, i.e., mall sales.

The next question you may ask is how much should an emergency fund be? Many financial mentors will tell you to build an amount of at least 5-6 months total of your monthly salary. It must be so you can have a budget enough for 5-6 months. For example, you will have enough budget for 5-6 months while looking for another job or establishing a business. Again, if you are earning a gross amount of 20,000 pesos per month then you need to multiply this amount by 5-6 times. Twenty thousand multiplied by six times amounts to 120,000 pesos. So, you need to build this amount in a bank. You should never touch this amount unless in a very, very urgent situation. Then whatever amount spent must be replenished as soon as possible.

How is an emergency fund built? Again, just like what I described earlier on saving, build your emergency fund slowly but surely. Set aside 5-10% (not absolute, you can adjust it to 20% or even higher) of your monthly salary and deposit it regularly into this fund. Taking once more the monthly salary of twenty thousand pesos. Ten percent of this is 2,000. You need to regularly set aside 2,000 pesos every month for five years to save the amount of 120,000 pesos as your emergency fund. Strictly follow this until the amount is built and let it stay in the bank. Adjust the amount of deposits when your salary increases. You can build your emergency fund while setting aside an amount for investing if your income and budget allow it.

In building your emergency fund, you need to impose very strict discipline on yourself. Build it as fast you can by depositing additional amounts once you receive additional bonuses so that the length of time in building it will be shortened. In this way, you have an earlier time to save and invest.

Once you finished creating your emergency fund, just let it stay there. Some people declare their emergency funds in time deposits to earn higher interest, but this is not advisable because its purpose is defied. Emergency funds usually do not earn high interest because it sits in the bank but remember that an emergency fund should be an emergency fund and do not use it anywhere! If you have none, any investments you make will be useless in case an emergency arrives because there is a very high possibility that you will prematurely withdraw your investments and divert to that urgent need.

c. **<u>SAVE and INVEST</u>**

Now it's time to save and invest. Many financial counselors again would advise you not to save literally but rather save and invest. There's a difference between "saving" and "saving and investing." Saving is just merely putting aside an amount of earning accumulating it in a bank or in your vaults. Usually, however, savings do not earn higher interests. On the other hand, saving and investing are different since you regularly set a portion of your salary (save) purposely for investing and the amount saved regularly is also invested regularly. It may be in cooperatives, PAG-IBIG funds, mutual funds, stocks, bonds, UITFs, and businesses where your money will multiply. I'm not an expert on these monetary terminologies so I will not discuss each of them in detail. What I would like to point out is about the knowledge and practice of putting aside a fraction of your regular salary even if it is small and consistently INVEST it.

One thing I would like to emphasize is: investing is for LONG TERM PURPOSES! Purposes like funds for building a house, something to use after mandatory retirement from work, an educational fund for your young children, etc. You must condition your mind that once you invest your money, you will get it back 10 to 20 years after when it has grown many, many times more than the capital. One of my favorite financial authors in the stock market says that "if you invest, forget about it and remember it only when you wake up after ten times an hour."

d. **BUY an INSURANCE**

One of the sensible decisions in life while young is to start buying life insurance. The earlier you start, the better, because you have more time to build your wealth and savings. For most young people especially if you are just 20 years old, the word "insurance" does not yet get well with your vocabulary. What is sad but the truth in Filipinos is that when one reaches 40 and above when illness strikes, then insurance becomes so appealing. Although if you are in the government, you are obliged to pay a monthly fee for GSIS but do you think that would suffice? While young, it is still wise to buy insurance from a legal and well-established company though you must explore your budget first if there's enough to cover more important options. Always be cautious though when selecting what corporation to engage with. Warning: do not ever transact with life insurance agents in malls! Transact only with the company itself at their legitimate offices. Be wary of scammers these days because of their tenacity as well as their very attractive modus operandi that is sometimes difficult to discern.

First of all, what is life insurance? This is a contract between the client who is principally the breadwinner and the life insurance company that states that the client will pay the company and when you die, the company will give your family or beneficiaries the sum of all your payments plus the interests. Insurance can act either as a financial security measure for your loved ones or as your retirement fund once you reach the age. The rewards of life insurance can only be attained after several years so you should expect to play the long game.

I recommend you read or listen or watch legitimate books, podcasts, or videos on how to grow/invest your money by legitimate and renowned Filipino financial speakers and authors. Why? You can relate immediately to the financial environment these authors and speakers are talking about including the different behavior patterns of Filipinos about money. Some authors, coaches, and or speakers I can mention here are Rex Ma. A. Mendoza CEO of Rampver Financials, Bo Sanchez of the Truly Rich Club, Edward Lee the founder of COL Financial Philippines, Marvin Germo a stock market trader, Chinkee Tan a wealth motivational speaker, Randell Tiongson an advocate of life and personal finance, Izza Glino a blogger on financial freedom, Fitz Villafuerte of the RFP Philippines and many others. It's recommended also to read books by or listen to famous non-Filipino financial mentors like Warren Buffet, Elon Musk, Tim Cook, Jack Ma, Robert Kiyosaki, and many more. You only have to brace yourself of the overwhelming inspirations they impart since many times readers will just pick up their teachings and shelf somewhere in the corners of their brains without actually putting these teachings into practice. This is because these authors are addressing people in the global arena. They do not know the typical behaviors of Filipinos and the environment of Philippine laws when it comes to monetary matters.

Setting your mindset or thinking paradigm

When it comes to money, people tend to become so irrational in many, many aspects even if they agree 150% that saving is a brilliant move. They still go for a buying spree once they receive their income or bonuses until nothing is left. I was like that before. Everybody knows that it's excellent to save but only a few do it. What should you do then? It takes an extra effort to tell yourself and rewire your brain to strictly follow a budgetary plan according to your income. Aiming for something to happen in the future takes preparation that includes some comforts to be sacrificed, e.g., dining out, travels, vacations, new gadgets, new clothes, extravagant spending.

You may not be aware yet of the behaviors of Filipinos and you may be one when it comes to money matters so let me describe them here:

a.   Behavior # 1

Income - Expenses = Savings

This is a common practice that everybody does. Upon receipt of salary, all bills including groceries, clothing, luxuries are deducted. Whatever is left becomes the savings. This too was my formula ever since I knew money. Most of the time though, nothing is left to save.

During months when bonuses are given especially the month of December when Christmas is also celebrated, Filipinos spend a lot on food and materials. Bank ATMs usually go short of cash because everybody needs to spend every centavo left. The reason I always hear about this yearend month is, "Christmas comes only once a year, so why not enjoy and give gifts." Filipinos also have that common term of "saving" for Christmas time. As if there is not another year to celebrate and as if this is the only reason to save every year but not to save for the longer-term future.

b.   Behavior # 2

Expense - Income = Debt

This behavior is ironically 'powerful' because even without receiving the income, it is already spent! For daily wage earners, I commonly hear the Filipino word, 'bale' which means bought on credit. They request an advance payment from their bosses and when the time comes to receive wages, they again request another advance payment. This will eventually lead to debt. For people who can afford to have credit cards, it means the same! Only, the scope of where to spend in advance is greater. Some say that a credit card is a *sinful card* because the temptation to swipe is so high as if you will never run out of money! If you never guard your spending, then you end up with a wide mouth trying to figure out why your debt is already higher than your income!

c.   Behavior # 3

Income - Savings = Expenses

This behavior is an idyllic one, but most Filipinos generally do not know it exists. It is a formula requiring one to deduct first and foremost whatever amount set as savings upon receipt of income or salary and whatever is left is used for expenses. This behavior is so difficult to put into practice if one is not so dedicated to doing it. It is a formula that generally everybody is alienated with much more with young professionals today.

For religious people who are active in their churches, this formula has an additional item to be deducted from the income, so the formula goes this way:

Income - Tithes - Savings = Expenses

d.   Behavior # 4

Income - Investments = Expenses

This behavior on money is not a new one but a revision of behavior # 3 as suggested by Mr. Edward Lee, the founder of COL Financial Philippines. As I explained earlier, saving should not be saving per se but saving an amount that you should use to invest. As to how much should you save to invest, the rule of thumb is any amount BUT should be an EXCESS of your budget.

Another rule of thumb is: DO NOT ever, ever borrow money to invest. Do not pounce on offers of loans to start a business. Loans will pull you surely to the drainage. While you may start earning, you also continuously pay the interest of your loan capital. And when will that stop? This is the reason why many financial gurus teach people to start small.

If you ask me how can we help Filipinos break the behavior numbers 1 and 2? This cannot be easily remedied. It will take maybe decades with the initiation of the Philippine government itself in the education system. And this will start by training first the young people's minds and inculcate in them the formula of saving and investing. Teaching the young professionals also on how to find other sources of income and controlling expenses will be a good move. These young people will eventually have families of their own and will soon teach their children of financial literacy and hope the cycle would move on.

How Do Controlling Expenses Work?

If you can't control how you spend, earning more or having multiple incomes will never help. You can only control what is going out or how much you spend. The way you handle a ten thousand income will be the same way you handle a hundred thousand income. In short, it's the way how you handle your income.

Manners on handling income that should be controlled (as inspired by Randell Tiongson):

a.	Don't go broke trying to look rich. Act based on your wage. For government employees, they are always reminded of what the Civil Service Commission reminds, 'to live within your means." Though food and clothing are among the fundamentals of survival, spending too much on them will lead to sick pockets.

b.	Don't fear investing in legitimate investments. Don't just keep your money in your vaults. Money not invested eventually becomes money spent. There are a lot of financial platforms that exist today, i.e., stock market, UITFs, Bonds, Mutual Funds, etc.

c.	Remove greed because it ultimately leads to financial failures. One of the lines spoken in the 1987 film, 'Wall Street" declares that "greed, for lack of a better word, is good."

I disagree! Greed has never had a positive effect. Greed is not good at all! It is the source of all financial foolishness and is the reason why many become irrational ultimately falling down the gutter to scams! Because of the urgent desire to increase money a hundred-fold in a very short time which is promised by all scammers will people get trapped. That temptation because of the desire to have the money urgently is a form of greed. Always remember that Wealth from get-rich-quick schemes quickly disappears too while work from hard work grows over time and not overnight. Time is a great ally.

If you are a religious Christian or from any faith, then your holy Books are sources of great inspiration for money advice. There are a lot of verses or sections, whatever they are called, that encourage or teach people not to be greedy and should be wise enough in handling money. Use the money for a greater goal. Filipinos are generous, but we do not have enough money to always give. Give to family, give to friends. Change. Use models. Listen to mentors who are very, very important. Be teachable. Implement.

d.   Ignorance. This attitude prevents you from making good decisions. Financial education is a big key to removing ignorance on money affairs. A lot has already been trapped in scams to the extent that even educated people defend organizations or groups promoting scams. Some leaders who had very clean intentions thus organizing what they call 'finance help hubs' get charged for criminal offenses is because of sheer ignorance. They didn't know what financial terms and definitions they were using to run their organizations. These usually grow so big and popular in the very short term. With that characteristic, should already be a red flag to you. In the Philippines, scam organizations continually evolve. Sadly, thousands believe in these forms of thefts who often tear up in the end! When will Filipinos ever learn when it comes to promises of swindling?

People of all walks get scammed! Why? They easily believe in the hypnotizing and golden promises of charlatans in the world of embezzlements. This is because of plain ignorance of financial literacy. In this digital age, defrauders are not that easy to recognize even what they are posting on social media. I am not against cryptocurrency, stock markets, U-markets, forex trading, insurances, and other paperless investments because these are legitimate platforms, but one must be always on guard of deceptions. Many are lured into these boards and eventually get scammed because of plain ignorance! I need to emphasize to you, young people that before engaging in any serious investments, you need to fully know or understand the room you are entering! Scrutinize their programs and objectives first if they are legal.

CHAPTER FOUR

THE FINANCIALLY LITERATE YOUNG FILIPINO PROFESSIONAL

"A formal education will make you a living; self-education will make you a fortune." — Jim Rohn

One financial advisor said, 'having NO MONEY is the greatest thing to be at!' This is because you will be forced to start small. It is here that you are teachable, become humble, and are willing to learn while doing your thing. On the other hand, people who have money tend to start Big then eventually FAIL because they have that ego of being monied. "I will put up a business when I retire so I will use my retirement money." "I will build my house if I retire." These are common announcements that employees say. Good if it would be so. But the majority cannot do it because either they have no money anymore because of debt already deducted from separation pay or pensions or they are already paying for medical expenses. So sad but the truth.

How important is it to have financial education?

Life now in conjunction with advancing technology corresponds to a lot of bills to pay. Every move takes an amount pulled out from pockets. Thus, a need to maintain a steady source of income. But how? A survey made by the BSP in 2019 reveals that only 29% of Filipinos have bank savings. This data is worrisome as it means that in the event of an emergency, a majority have empty pockets. This also indicates that Filipinos could fall into debt or worse, not be able to pay emergency bills.

Since March 2020 the Philippines has been experiencing widespread unemployment. Our economy being reinforced by remittances of almost 10 million OFWs has also been affected because of limited economic activities in other countries due to lockdowns caused by the pandemic.

World Remit country-director Earl Melivo believes that the Philippine government should have a multidimensional and extensive approach to increase the financial literacy of Filipino citizens. "It would be a long way to go," he said, but if not started will end up nothing. Further, Melivo emphasized that "financial literacy should be deeply embedded very early on in our educational system from the secondary level through to the university level. Financial literacy must start at a young age, including the importance of savings, wise use of credit, and the presence of both traditional and digital financial services in the country." I was so glad to note that true to Melivo's statement, the DepEd has issued its Financial Education Policy in July 2021 under DepEd Order No. 022 Series of 2021. Through the Bureau of Curriculum Development (BCD), DepEd has intensified the integration of financial literacy in the basic education curriculum of the K-12 which was a brilliant move. Pursuant to this, RA No. 10922 known as the "Economic and Financial Literacy Act" was enacted on July 27, 2015, declaring the Second Week of November of Every Year as Economic and Financial Literacy Week aimed towards developing a national consciousness on the economic and financial literacy of which majority are not aware of its existence. Section 2 of the Act declares that "the State recognizes the growth potential of the country through financially literate people who make sound financial decisions, mobilize savings, and contribute ideas on improving economic and financial policies and programs." I, for one, am very grateful for this step in our education system. It has a long way to go but at least the journey has begun.

What is it that keeps Filipinos saving so much in difficulty? There's a good lot of possible answers but one general argument may be the easy-go-lucky attitude of many. The majority of Filipinos lack discipline and commitment to remain on the road of savings and investments including building an emergency fund. After all, it means giving up a portion of the regular income and habitually committing to it while resisting the urge to let loose the spending evils in mind. It is so extremely challenging for most.

Let's examine some of the 6 most common reasons why Filipinos are so unwilling to save and how to possibly curtail it yourself. If these apply to you then push yourself to take the first step and figure out how to leave these bad attitudes behind:

1.   'Bahala na' attitude. This is one of the most dangerous mindsets that most Filipinos have, by leaving finances to fate. Going to a battle without any preparation will surely put one immediately running back for dear life.

I had friends during my youth who chose to get married at a very early age. Out of sheer frankness sometimes, I boldly asked them why they had to get married that soon and how could they go to college or how would they continue their degrees. All their responses were, 'bahala na!" This had been also my attitude though not in getting married early but in many aspects in life that I needed to face a decision. Most of the time I depended on fate alone and kept on praying that everything would go right after. What if it didn't!

The 'bahala na' attitude will not always end you up to the best if talking about finances because you need to prepare so you will not hang on to luck!

Management Approach:

Getting started can be really hard but your best motivation could be a future with peace of mind of having something you have prepared for. Since you aim to improve your financial life, then, do your part first by conditioning your mind to be committed to saving a small portion of your income. You want to be financially independent. You want to be worry-free when you get older.

Cross your fingers with me and promise yourself to commit to this determination to improve your financial situation. You may opt to consult other financial professionals on the decisions that are available for you. Doing the action is far, far safe than just putting your future to the uncertain. So, act now. Get a marker and a nice notebook to pen all your plans and daily actions on your finances.

2.   Not knowing how to save. Most people agree that saving is a good thing, but

they find it horribly difficult to practice it. It seems impossible to say that some still do not know how to save. Well, everybody knows how to do it, and no one can argue with me that it's an excellent move. Even a 5-year old child when taught knows how to save. It's basic knowledge. One doesn't have to be a college graduate to know how to save part of an income. It's just your commitment to yourself. The choice is up to you.

I always despise the belief of many Filipinos that it's an omen to save because you are preparing for sickness or death. This belief usually pulls away most from the habit of saving. If you understand the sense of having a dream, a goal, care for tomorrow then shake off those negative vibrations.

Management Approach:

There are a lot of saving tips on the internet today. Be sure only to select those that are legitimate. Anyway, before you start saving, I need to ask you first if you are currently in debt. Because if so, then you must gradually pay first all your debts so that you can be free to move around with your finances and save. Just like what I did, I had to fully pay my strings of debts in five years! Imagine that five years of just paying debt! It was no fun, but I was determined to get out of debt. And I did it. Figure out how much you should pledge to regularly save and go open a bank account. It is highly recommended that you use a passbook and not ATM so that you won't have easy access to it. There is a wide range of savings accounts or instruments today, depending on your time horizon and risk appetite.

3.   Not having enough money left for savings. Creating more reasons not to start saving even a single peso a day will place you in a fate of nothingness. Not having enough money is the sole reason Filipinos do not seriously commit themselves to saving because of some sub-reasons like being buried in debt. They argue that they need to pay-off first their debts. In many cases, debts are non-ending as well with not saving forever.

This mindset will keep you from starting to save and when an emergency strikes, the usual thing to do is to have additional loans. If you are receiving a regular salary, then it would be impossible to say that you have no money for savings! It doesn't mean that you need to have a hundred thousand salary per month before you can be able to say that you have enough money already to save. No matter how big or small a salary is, if received regularly, then there's no reason not to save enough.

Management Approach

If you are earning P16,000 to P20,000 per month and you cannot yet put aside a regular monthly amount of P500.00 then that would be a sad story after all. The Philippine government had become lenient in deducting taxes to wage earners having below P20,000.00 a month of tax exemption so there's no reason not to sacrifice even a P500.00 as savings. The rule of thumb is always to PAY YOURSELF FIRST. You may ask, how to start. First, pledge yourself an amount to keep so consistently every payday or every month. If you are receiving P26,000 per month then save 10% of it that means 2,600 per month. And I repeat, make a regular deposit into a bank using a passbook and not an ATM. If this seems so straining because you are currently paying debts, then you might as well just concentrate on paying your debt first. But if your income allows, then start at 5% which means you need to set aside P1,300 a month while paying your debt. Make it a serious habit. Again, make it a serious habit! Remember, that the amount you are saving is for yourself so you must have that dignity of discipline to commit to this task. If it needs to be that you must give up some expenses especially if not so necessary, then do it! To save, it is important to plan for how you will save and make it a part of your budget. Therefore, it is important to have a budget that will guide you with your spending, and that will help you to minimize unnecessary expenses. Make a simple spreadsheet or a list to help you keep your budget in check. To add, if you go to groceries, make sure to have a list of what you are going to buy. Do not ever attempt to place unlisted items into your cart. It's currently a sin while you are saving and rolling out from debts.

4.	Fearing the unknown. Fear prevents one from grabbing good opportunities. This is one emotion that when nurtured will lead one to nothingness. One of the sources of fear is the handed down make beliefs that the younger generation also believes even if without a scientific basis. For example, saving is an omen because it means you are preparing for a bad event to happen. This is a great lie from the negative force ushering you to a life of difficulty.

Management Approach:

Remember that you are now a professional and have taken subjects in human behavior, for sure Psychology and some sciences. Teach yourself of vibrations that will equate your life to higher ground. Do not believe in making beliefs but believe in facts that would help you in very positive feedback. Facts are grounds where you can play and establish your financial powers and not in fearing the unknown.

5.   Always protecting ego or self-handicapping. This behavior is one among those pushing people to financial downfall. Ego prevents you from learning from others and sabotages your chances of success. Yes, we all want to feel good about ourselves but going beyond to avoid taking responsibility for our failures would hurt our chances of success. Self-handicapping though can be an effective strategy for protecting self-esteem, but this can have a significantly negative impact on success. Protecting your ego is a self-sabotaging action or choice that prevents you from taking personal responsibility for consequences. One may create barriers so that any possible failures can then be blamed on the outside forces. Failure becomes more painful when realizing that lack of preparation leads to a more sober consequence. For example, students may put off studying until the last minute. Athletes may skip practice before the competition and then resort to drugs/steroids a night before the big day. Or in another scenario is, an athlete may have been preparing for an event but would find doubting his ability to successfully win the

game during the competition. Another is, going to mall sales with friends who are extravagant spenders ending you up to spend what you all tried to save because you didn't want to show your friends that you are out of order leaving the mall without something bought.

Management Approach

First, go out to a quiet place, maybe in your room, where you will possibly be alone. Sit down and pull a few moments to assess yourself. Open your mind to your own by not involving someone to blame but you and you, alone. Second, ask yourself and say, 'what if?' 'What if I will do this to help me', 'to help me get out of debt,' 'what if I will invest, etc.' Go the extra mile to help yourself start what you planned. Learn also to say, 'no' if it is necessary. Saying no will not kill you.

6.   Cultivating envy. Envy is very dangerous behavior because this can result in a very horrible consequence. This is one form of insecurity! Envy prevents you from focusing

on yourself from achieving financial freedom. If you keep on eyeing what your neighbors are doing, you will end up with nothing. For example, buying a car ends you up in compounded loans, buying expensive gadgets, designer bags, clothing, shoes, etc. just because your friends or enemies or your neighbors have it. It may be very difficult at the start to stop yourself from getting envious, but you need to have a positive determination and tell yourself that envy begets dishonesty and malevolence. In this way, you can help your mind shift to a positive and peaceful state.

Management Approach

There are a lot of self-help books and e-books or advice from YouTube, podcasts, etc. Try to read or listen to them and apply the step-by-step guide on freeing your mind from envy. Be serious and open your heart to the methods. You must start with yourself by counting first your blessings. You have so many blessings unique to you. Then start replacing envy with clear actions. Just focus on

yourself. Plan for your life and start building
now.

CHAPTER FIVE
OVERCOMING FINANCIAL NORMS THAT HINDER ONE TO SAVE AND INVEST

"Before you can become a millionaire, you must learn to think like one. You must learn how to motivate yourself to counter fear with courage."
—Thomas J. Stanley

"Our goals can only be reached through a vehicle of a plan, in which we must fervently believe, and upon which we must vigorously act. There is no other route to success." — Pablo Picasso

Saving is the first step towards ensuring your financial health. Therefore, you must put an end to the endless excuses and get into the savings habit now. Stop the notion that saving is a duty and don't think of it as something you can do tomorrow when you have more money because tomorrow is surely infinity. Remember, the money you save NOW ensures a more secure future for you and the people you love. Try getting off on the following abnormal norms:

1. Going All-Out for One-time or One-day events. Many Filipinos are afraid of what their neighbors might say when they do not celebrate birthdays, weddings, debuts, and other celebrations extravagantly. They feel so pressured to the extent that some people avail of loans just to finance these celebrations. Many times, this attitude puts many into a situation where they get into more trouble of being buried deeper in debt just to save their faces from the shame of not celebrating an occasion. It would be best to celebrate within one's means, even if that would mean a conservative feast. After all, we don't want to have one memorable day followed by years of suffering.

2. Using Credit cards for non-essentials. This tiny card is considered an advertising machine. If possible, cut those credit cards and put them all into the waste bin. Buy your needs in cash and never use those cards again. If it's very difficult to get off that credit card from

your wallets, then maintain only one but ask your bank to issue you a new one that has a credit limit of 15% of your monthly salary or lower. Then always promptly pay the whole amount of dues. Do not just pay the down payment. This is to avoid arrears. Note however that this credit card should only be used strictly in emergency cases for example when you cannot immediately go to a bank for cash. Discipline yourself not to use it when roaming the malls or when surfing the internet.

3. High-status symbols. Another abnormal norm is buying things that are not immediate needs. This is a problem common to many government employees. Once they occupy a position which means their salaries are also upgraded, they start thinking of many things out of priorities or not basic needs. For example, cars, gadgets, or expensive appliances/ equipment like an expensive camera for hobbies are not converted to money. What is more disappointing to note is that these non-priorities are acquired from a mortgage.

Another status symbol is overspending for house designs and decors. And another more is house acquisition for long years of the loan (i.e., housing programs of 20-25 years loan) and purchasing a huge house that requires regular maintenance.

4. Student loans lead to long-term debts. Currently not a large practice yet in the Philippines unlike in most countries in the West although some government entities had been offering this kind before with a partner bank. The scheme was called Study Now Pay Later Plan. This was my case when I was finishing my second year in college. There were slots for this program in our university and I got one. The mortgagee was a government insurance system with their chosen partner government banks. Three months after I graduated, I was sent a notice from the bank that I need to pay what I borrowed. Of course, the lender was a bank so naturally, it had interest added. Today, there are a lot of scholarships offered to young people. Besides, Philippine education

embarked on free tuition in the entire levels in all government schools, so what more?

5. The belief is that investing is not for everyone. This is a sad assumption common to many Filipinos. Many believe that investing is only for someone destined to do it. If you immerse yourselves immediately in this kind of mindset then you cannot start any investment. Where do you commonly immerse yourselves at? Isn't it on where and what to buy, buy, buy not thinking of where to save, save, save and invest? Remember that anyone can do saving and invest. It is simple!

Succeed as an Employee, Entrepreneur, and Investor

Being an employee is not bad at all. We all need a source of income. What is bad is when you are an employee and stay as one forever without thinking of investing even a small amount. Here are simple steps that you can follow as an employee and becoming an entrepreneur and investor:

1.   Start with a perspective.

Most Filipino employees have money for luxuries but none to save for investment. Their mindsets have already been nailed into buying and buying without thinking if what they are buying will give them back something for additional income.

As early as now, cultivate the discipline or habit of saving first and then investing. Expand your horizon or income potentials. Use weekends and holidays or a few hours after 5:00 p.m. to do online business or any income-generating ventures. Do not rely solely on your salaries especially since you are still young in your careers and it is understood that your monthly income is not yet that much. It is so sad to note that most Filipinos especially young professionals today spend 3 hours a day wasted on social media, TV, watching YouTube. Spending more time on these avenues is longer on weekends. And if we compute this number of hours per day in a week x 30 days x 12 months in a year would be too much of a waste.

One way of investing is through the Philippine Stock Exchange, Inc. It's a stock market. The nature of the stock market in the earlier years was millions to invest. Now, 50 to 1,000 pesos is possible as the initial investment. If you save today as young as you are and use it as capital to invest, this will generate money for you in the long term.

Principles of Long-term investment

Only 8% of Filipinos prepare for the long-term according to the BSP. Filipinos generally rely on their SSS and GSIS but are this enough! A lot of Filipinos struggle so much when it comes to money. There are so many factors in every Filipino home why this scenario is so common. We have very close-knit family ties. In the mind of every first child in a Filipino family, has equal responsibility with the parents subconsciously integrated. Once the first child gets employed, has to share with the family budget including the sending of younger siblings to school. Added to this even is the responsibility to give to close relatives.

2.   Time Management.

I frequently get amused by someone I know who holds a Ph.D. degree, and is even a professor addressing graduate students in her fold and fiercely insisting that time can be managed! Well, it cannot be. You can never manage TIME because time is there ticking every nanosecond up to infinity! What you can only manage is YOURSELF! Now, I want to address the youth that you need to manage yourselves and be productive while you are young because you and I can never bring back time. Once it's gone, it's gone! Don't dilly-dally and remember that tomorrow will never end but your life will. Practice leadership skills. You know, I always get several questions in mind if how world-changers and successful people ever manage themselves and get productive without so much impact on their health. I get to tell myself that they are crazy! Well, this is because of their passion and love that drives them on what they are accomplishing in life. They have that internal and external structure in mind to follow.

3. Having multiple sources of income even if you are a government employee

When I transferred to the academe, I carried with me some practices that I did at my former workplace about a very modest product dealership activity. The scheme was on a commission basis. It was just something like most do by carrying with them a few items in their bags and showing to friends or colleagues involving ladies' personal consumables or packaged snacks. I usually did things like this during noon breaks or after office hours because I knew it was forbidden by the Civil Service Commission to be doing such activities while on government duty. There was no Facebook nor Twitter nor Instagram, etc. during those years to plug in advertisements. During my first two years in the new job, I was bullied by a professor who called my attention two times of doing 'moonlighting,' (a term of doing extra source of income aside from the main job without the supervisor knowing it) and pointing at me by words: 'Is your salary not enough? 'Choose!

Stay as an instructor or continue your moonlighting!' I was spotted showing a product to a colleague during lunchtime. That professor was not even my boss! Anyway, what I wanted to reiterate on this unfortunate incident was the statement, 'not enough salary.' As I described in Chapter One, the salaries of most government employees are way below the poverty line. Unless you receive salary grades equivalent to a hundred thousand pesos and above per month then you may comfortably say that your salary is enough. But enough is not enough yet depending on the lifestyle one carries.

I encourage the young professionals today to have multi-sources of income. It's not illegal to have some economic sources. Never rely on your very own salaries because it is not enough! You have holidays, weekends, and time after 5:00 in the afternoon. Do something worthwhile to create other sources of income. This generation has all the offers of advertisements that were not available 5-10 years ago. Product advertisements are all available online and you can just find any platform where you can plug in your business. I only would want to warn you that you do this additional income-generating outside these office hours which are from 8:00 a.m. to 12:00 noon and 1:00 p.m. to 5:00 p.m. Of course, you will be reprimanded or charged with administrative cases if you bring with you your extra source of income to your official workplace advertising or using official hours.

4. Practice the 70-20-10 Principle of Budgeting

When you spend without a plan, it's easy to quickly blow through your money with no relief until the next payday. A lack of a solid money management strategy can often be the culprit. That's where the 70-20-10 budgeting method comes in to disrupt that paycheck-to-paycheck cycle. The 70-20-10 budget is a percentage-based money management style that helps you make room for saving and investing and even paying your debts and donating. The 70% will be for your living expenses, 20% for savings, and 10% for investing. You may notice that investing is only

10% so it can be done. However, this 10% can either be for investing, tithing, donations. Saving is even 20% which can be doable. This percentage allocation is not absolute. It can be adjusted. This principle only offers you guidance on how to start managing your income or money. If you exceed in any category, then reduce your spending in the other areas. If you want to put more money into your savings, then you must reduce your living expenses. Let's put this into a real example. The current starting salary of most young professionals in the government is around P26,000.00. Since the rule of thumb is to set aside first and foremost the percentage for savings of 20%, then immediately set aside 5,200.00 plus the 10% for an investment of 2,600.00. The total is 7,800.00. The remaining 70% is now 18,200.00. You can now spend this on your bills, groceries, food, etc. However, since our example of a monthly income of 26,000.00, this is taxable under the Philippine law of roughly 8-10%. So, if the tax is 2,300.00 then this amount is lessened from the 70% for living expenses to amount to 15,860.00 instead of 18,200.00.

In 2017, under a revised proposal, Filipinos with a monthly income of P21,000 or below are exempted from paying personal income tax, generating over P21,000 in savings annually. This is among the tax reform plans of the government in close coordination with the Department of Finance (DOF). So, if your salary belongs to this category then you can play around the 70-20-10 budgeting rule without tax.

In addition, to be able to stick to this budgeting principle, you may find the following helpful:

a. Track your monthly expenses by listing down first your daily expenses employing a daily planner. Then by using a spreadsheet, plot these expenses so you can easily determine where you are spending most. For example, if your biggest expense is on food, then you may consider cutting down on that area. If on decorations, clothing, other unnecessary items, then consider the items if they are badly necessary. You may cut down large expenses on these.

b. Increase your income by engaging in investments and other small businesses.

c. Practice **Income** minus **Savings/Investments** equals **Expenses** (Income – Savings = Expenses)

d. Pay off your debt with a determined spirit.

e. Reduce household and miscellaneous expenses. There are a lot of things out there that you think you need inside the house but actually would just end up in storage rooms or corners. This is the reason why you are encouraged to go to grocery stores or malls with a list on hand. Most of the time, especially for ladies, cute yet pricey little decors are too tempting. But are you sure you badly need those items?

f.	Practice minimalism now. Being a minimalist – knowing exactly what you want and avoiding accumulating things that you don't need – will surely save you from having huge expenses. Instead of putting your money on useless items that would soon accumulate dust, it's best to wisely invest in paper assets that will surely benefit you after 20 years.

EPILOGUE

Financial literacy is still the best tool to effectively divert many from the pangs of debt. Planning for retirement while very young is not bad at all. There are many platforms today where anyone can join and be educated about personal finances and where anyone can do investments. Saving is an imperative move to improve individual and societal welfare. At the personal level, saving helps households achieve efficient spending patterns.

Owing to a positive mindset, teaching financial literacy to young people provides solutions to financial problems. And while saving, be watchful also in safeguarding your money. Although saving is now taught in schools and various meetings, policymakers still need to look into teaching people the possibility of saving more by paying down existing debts. In the Philippines, the current administration has been taking small steps to pin down the problem of debts and encouraging everyone to save more to have an excess amount to be invested. Investing in stock markets and mutual funds for example does not anymore require huge amounts as an initial investment but 500 to 1,000 pesos can do with even minimum charges. Paper assets are now non-taxable to encourage Filipinos to save and invest on these kinds of platforms.

Since there is a rising number of senior-dependents or those retirees who depend on their children for financial help, due to lack of financial education, orienting young people today regarding financial planning can help them to break the cycle. In this way, these individuals will know how to be responsible when it comes to their finances and instill the discipline needed to keep track of their financial goals.

On the other hand, while living in this world of complexities, it's always wise to be wary of what you are planning for the future to avoid being scammed. A spirit of discernment especially on finances must be cultivated. Being serious in increasing income while joining investment platforms, remodeling of the brain first to remove greed is a must while carving this piece of advice into your mind: 'Raise your financial IQs' so that you will not be trapped by the modus operandi of scammers. Learn to spot dangers before they come to you. Since everyone has a brain, use it to think, study and do research of the system being offered. Once a recruiter comes and offers a GUARANTEED HIGH RETURNS in a very short while, immediately stay away! That's already a red flag to anyone to stand back no matter how enticing the promise is. There are so many victims because of this 'assurance.' What is so sad is that professionals and even rich people fall prey to these scammers. Victims get instantly blinded by this false promise. Always remember that investing to earn high revenues entails a process. It does NOT occur overnight.

"A dream doesn't become reality through magic; it takes sweat, determination and hard work."
— Colin Powell

ABOUT THE AUTHOR

 **Yoli Angeles** has a Bachelor of Science degree in Agriculture from the Benguet State University. She worked as a government employee for over 20 years. Her own financial struggles compelled her to write this book, which she believes will inspire every young Filipino professional and employee to save and invest. Yoli is currently an Associate Professor but at the same time, she is also a financial counselor to millennial employees and young professionals.

A GIFT FOR YOU

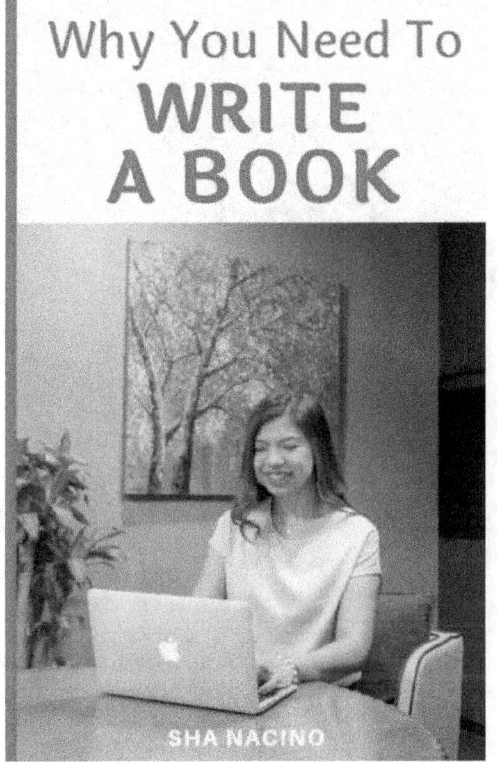

To download this free eBook, simply go to
TheAuthorsVoice.net/book

ARE YOU A YOUNG PROFESSIONAL?

If your answer is YES,
then this book is for YOU!

My Wallet After 20 Years will help you realize the importance of financial literacy and how essential it is to manage your financial resources early on. This book provides a step-by-step approach to managing income and guides you on how to invest for the future.

ABOUT THE AUTHOR

Yoli Angeles is an Associate Professor with a passion for financial mentoring. She witnessed several employees end up in tough situations because they lacked financial wisdom.

She had been in a similar circumstance as an employee. This motivated her to take action in order to encourage new young Filipino professionals today to save and invest.

www.ingramcontent.com/pod-product-compliance
Lightning Source LLC
Chambersburg PA
CBHW061249140726
47998CB00006B/2161